DADS
do
Breakfast

Donald B. Gioffre

LifeRich Publishing books may be ordered through booksellers or by contacting:

LifeRich Publishing
1663 Liberty Drive
Bloomington, IN 47403
www.liferichpublishing.com
1 (888) 238-8637

Because of the dynamic nature of the Internet, any web addresses or links contained in this book may have changed since publication and may no longer be valid. The views expressed in this work are solely those of the author and do not necessarily reflect the views of the publisher, and the publisher hereby disclaims any responsibility for them.

Any people depicted in stock imagery provided by Thinkstock are models, and such images are being used for illustrative purposes only.
Certain stock imagery © Thinkstock.

ISBN: 978-1-4897-0091-9 (sc)
ISBN: 978-1-4897-0090-2 (hc)
ISBN: 978-1-4897-0092-6 (e)

Library of Congress Control Number: 2013922363

Printed in the United States of America.

LifeRich Publishing rev. date: 04/03/2014

LifeRich
PUBLISHING
an imprint of The Reader's Digest Association, Inc.

Dads Do Breakfast

This world seems to have gone crazy right before our eyes   and our family relationships are paying the price. Statistics show that in the last 25 years the time parents spend with their children has dropped 40 percent. In a 24 hour period parents work on average 8.2 hours, watch 5.5 hours of TV or other media and spend 35 minutes on mobile devices, but they spend only a shocking two hours a day with their children.[1] These facts are not only startling but also disturbing.

Everyone admits it is a very fast, frenzied, and rather impersonal world we live in today. When you consider the intense schedules we set for ourselves and our families, one can easily see why there is little or no time left for quality family time. *Pressure* and *stress* abound everywhere!

Men, it is time that we do something to slow our lives down a little and take control of the most significant part of the day: *breakfast* (at least on Saturday or Sunday or both if you can). Breakfast is the most important meal of the day, and what could be better than sharing this with the most important people in your life? It will set the tone and spirit for the rest of your day!

Men, you can make a statement *forever* if you become the *breakfast master. It is easy, it is fun,* and it is oh so *important*. It seems that everywhere you look (especially in TV ads), the role of men is becoming minimized and trivialized. By doing *breakfast*, and doing it right, you can make an incredible statement and create lasting memories for your family.

It is great to get everyone involved in the preparations and even in the actual cooking. It is something they will take with them forever.

Our boys are grown now, with families of their own, but they still talk about our Sunday morning

---

1   Source: Part Eight: Parenting: Do Parents Know How Much Time They Spend with Their Children? 2000; Dr. Penelope Leach Institute for the Study of Children, Families and Social Issues; 2011; Source: American Time Use Survey 2011

omelets or pizza fritta, and our Magnolia Sunrise drinks (nonalcoholic for them at the time). These may be great memories for them, but to Renee and me, they are *priceless*.

Our grandchildren love Papa's scrambled eggs, and they are crazy about my Pizza Fritta Lungas together with Naenae's Potatoes and Eggs and her special-shaped pancakes. Breakfast in our family has become a time of love, laughter, and lots of fun.

This book contains many new recipes, staples, and of course lots of old favorites, some with a new twist. They are tasty, easy, and many times, absolutely *fabulous*. You can change most recipes to your particular diet or liking. You can take many shortcuts by buying some already prepared items. You can prepare many parts of the dishes ahead, thus making it much easier for yourself

Most importantly, don't be afraid; just do it. Get everyone in the kitchen. Give Mom the morning off. *It's time to get cooking.*

Remember, it doesn't have to be fancy, and it doesn't even have to be fabulous. *It just has to be done together!*

Dads Do Breakfast, and So Do Granddads

Sure, dads do breakfast but so do granddads, or at least we granddads should. It is even easier for us because we have a lot more time to prepare and are able to do so much more in advance. That's the beauty part because it makes preparing breakfast so much easier. Always remember to read your recipe through to the end before starting.

Many granddads don't see their children and grandkids as much as they would like. As granddads we can't do the things we used to. We can't walk on our hands anymore or run as fast as we used to. So when you do see your families, make the most of it. You can make some delicious breakfasts, but you can also make some *fun* breakfasts.

For instance, let's say the kids come to your house or you go to theirs for a birthday celebration. Make a nice stack of pancakes, and decorate them as you would a *birthday cake*. Use whipped cream, candles, and birthday decorations. You can also place a birthday hat on top.

You can turn the average pancake or waffle into exciting shapes or themes. There is an abundance of pancake molds available in many fun shapes. And for waffles, you can use regular cookie cutters to transform your waffles into magical shapes for your grandchildren. For added flair, serve these delightful treats with your grandchildren's favorite fruit or berries and topped with yummy whipped cream or syrups.

Come on, use your imagination or try looking through magazines for inspiration.

Just remember one thing: show your family just how much you *love* them. Kiss them, hug them, and make the best and most memorable breakfast they will ever have.

One more thing: *take lots and lots* of pictures and present them in a photo album that will be filled with a treasure of family memories.

Dad's Very Important Hints and Ideas

Dad knows that cooking may seem very difficult or at least intimidating for many men, so here are a few extremely important hints and some handy ideas that will help take the pressure off. It is also important to note that these hints will make it much easier to get started and follow through for a great breakfast for your family and friends.

- Read the whole recipe first. Then think the recipe through before you start. This can be done the night before. This will make it much easier to prepare and coordinate the breakfast.

- Prepare and lay out your ingredients and utensils before you start.

- Crack your eggs in a separate bowl or dish before you add them to other ingredients. This will make it easier to check for shells.

- It is important to taste as you go so you can adjust your seasoning and make sure everything tastes just right.

- Safety first—frying bacon splatters, so keep the kids at a safe distance and especially not at eye level to the stovetop.

- Eliminate any alcohol from a recipe the children may have. You can substitute any of several extracts to compensate for taste. Most of the recipes that call for liquor will do just fine without it.

- You can substitute almost any ingredients to suit your taste or dietary needs.

- You don't always have to fry your bacon. You can bake it in the oven. If you are in a rush, purchase a package of the precooked bacon from the supermarket. You just have to microwave the bacon and you're good to go. It's pretty tasty too.

- Use pancake molds for your pancakes to make special and fun shapes for the kids or for special occasions. You can also purchase a pancake batter dispenser to make this task easier and also allow you to create your own free-form shapes.

- Use whipped cream or syrups to make fun designs on top of your pancakes or waffles. And don't forget to use candles for birthdays.

- Try not to brown the butter when melting because it will cause a bitter taste and ruin your dish. If you do brown the butter, just carefully wipe it out and start over again. Adjust the heat so you won't burn it again.

- Purchase a heat-proof spatula.

- Test for doneness. For instance, when your scrambled eggs are wet and shiny but not runny, they are done, so remove them from the heat.

- Don't forget the appropriate music to set the stage for your special breakfast. For example, birthday, Hawaiian, special holiday music, etc.

- Don't forget your camera. The pictures you take today will provide memories that will last forever.

Last and most importantly, if you think the meal went wrong (didn't work out the way you wanted it to), *don't go crazy*. Take it easy; it's probably not as bad as you think, and your family probably won't even notice.

Remember, it's about being together. If you overreact, your family will remember that much more than a not-so-great meal. *You love them, so teach them great values first and how to cook second.*

Eggs

Frying eggs is very easy. Just follow these hints. Of course, add more ingredients for larger portions or more people.

Ingredients

2 eggs

2 tbsp. unsalted butter

Kosher salt and pepper to taste

2 slices of your favorite toast or English muffins

Heat a nonstick frying pan or skillet over medium-high heat. Let the pan get hot, and then lower the heat to medium. Add the butter, and swirl to coat the pan. I like to add a little extra butter.

Crack the eggs in a separate flat dish. If you don't want to use a separate dish, carefully crack the eggs just inches above the frying pan. Watch for shells. Add salt and pepper. Let the eggs set for two to three minutes. It is okay if the edges of the eggs get a little brown as they start to firm up.

At this point, spoon some of the melted butter over the top of the eggs. This will add more taste and help to cook the top of the eggs.

Your eggs should be finished now. If you like your eggs sunny sides down, slide a heat-proof spatula under the eggs one at a time, and gently flip them to the other side. Cook for thirty seconds more.

Slide the eggs out of the pan on to your plate. Serve with toast or English muffins.

In the movie *Midnight Run,* who could ever forget the famous words spoken by Charles Grodin to Robert DeNiro: "I want chorizo and eggs"? After a harried trip across the country, and desperately low on money, he was given the choice of several other specials, but with a down-and-out, deadpan voice, he would only say, "I want chorizo and eggs." No wonder—chorizo sausage and eggs are a great breakfast dish. You'll love it too, and it's so easy to make.

Ingredients

8 eggs

3 tbsp. butter

6 links chorizo sausage

4 tbsp. half and half or milk

Kosher salt and pepper

4 Portuguese rolls

2 tsp. cilantro or parsley, finely chopped

Heat a large skillet or frying pan over medium heat, and then add one tbsp. butter. Heat until the butter is melted. Slice the chorizo links into quarter- to half-inch slices and add to the heated pan. Cook the chorizo for about four to five minutes or until browned. Remove and set aside.

Whisk the eggs, half and half (or milk), salt, and pepper. Carefully wipe out the pan. Melt two tbsp. of butter over medium heat. Lower the heat and add the egg mixture to the pan, lifting and folding the eggs gently to form large curds. Halfway through the scrambling process (about two minutes), add the cooked chorizo sausage to the eggs.

Lift and fold the chorizo into the egg mixture and continue to cook for another one to two minutes.

As you are cooking the eggs and chorizo, split and lightly toast the Portuguese rolls. Add one half of each roll to a serving plate, and scoop the eggs and chorizo on top. Sprinkle some parsley or cilantro on top and serve.

Abrigado—thank you. Well done!

PS: *Midnight Run* (1988) is a great movie. Try to rent it, and then say, "I want chorizo and eggs." Don't settle for anything else.

A hearty breakfast to start the day out on the range is essential. The same goes for those of us heading out for a day of work or fun. This breakfast is rustic home cooking at its best. It is also an easy breakfast dish for the kids to help prepare.

Ingredients

8–10 eggs

1 cup ham, diced

3 tbsp. half and half

4 tbsp. butter

2 tbsp. corn oil

1 large russet potato, finely diced

1 large onion, sliced or chopped

½ cup Monterey Jack cheese, diced, sliced, or grated

Salt and pepper

2 tbsp. chives, minced

1 tbsp. Italian parsley, chopped

Heat a large cast iron skillet or nonstick frying pan over medium-high heat. Add butter and oil to the pan. When the butter is melted, add potato, onion, salt, and pepper to taste. Stir occasionally.

Cook until potatoes are tender and onions begin to caramelize, about ten minutes. Add ham and cook two minutes more, stirring occasionally.

Crack eggs into a bowl. Add half and half and salt and pepper to taste, and then whisk until well mixed. Reduce heat on potato mixture, and add eggs. As the eggs begin to set, gently stir in cheese, parsley, and chives. Lift the mixture with a heat-proof spatula to let uncooked eggs flow to bottom of the pan.

Continue to cook for two to three minutes more or until all of the egg is set. Slide completed eggs onto a serving plate, garnish with parsley, and serve.

The easiest and best way to make soft-boiled eggs is to prepare everything in advance. You will need a four- to six-quart saucepan with enough water to cover the eggs by about one to two inches. You will need four eggs at room temperature (two for each serving). You will also need a bowl filled with ice water large enough to fit the finished eggs without crowding them.

Place your eggs in the saucepan filled with at least two quarts of boiling water. Be careful, and place them in the pan very gently. Reduce the heat to medium, and let the eggs simmer for five minutes for soft, runny eggs or six minutes for firmer eggs.

Remove the eggs immediately with a large slotted spoon, and place them one by one into the ice bath for two minutes. Place the eggs in an egg cup or small cereal dish. Snip off the top of the eggshell and serve.

To make hard-boiled eggs, place the eggs in a pot with enough cold water to cover them by one inch, bring to a boil, remove pot from the heat, and let the eggs stand in the water for ten minutes.

Follow these three easy steps:

1. Fill a high-sided skillet or fairly large pan with water (leave some room for the egg and for boiling water). Bring the water to a boil. Add two teaspoons of white vinegar to the water and half a teaspoon of salt.

2. Crack an egg into a small dish, like a ramekin or cup. Reduce the heat to low.

3. Slowly slide the egg into the water and cook for three minutes for softer eggs and four minutes for a firmer egg. Remove the egg from the pan with a slotted spoon so all the water will drain. Serve over toast.

Eggs Three Ways is perfect for a last-minute or quick breakfast. It is also perfect because it will please almost anyone. Eggs Three Ways will just about guarantee that your family or friends will get their eggs their way.

Ingredients

4 eggs, or as many as desired
4 English muffins
4 slices ham*

Butter for frying eggs and buttering muffins
4 slices of Swiss cheese or your choice of cheese
Salt and pepper

To make Eggs Three Ways, you fry, scramble, or poach your eggs. Whichever you choose to please each guest, cook them as you normally would, keep warm, and set aside.

Meanwhile, split, toast, and butter your English muffins. Then set them aside and keep warm.

Place the bottom half of one muffin on each plate. Place egg, one slice of ham, and then one slice of cheese on top. Cover with the other half of the muffin.

Place the egg sandwich is a microwave for about thirty seconds, heat, remove, and serve.

You may substitute bacon or salmon for the ham.

This is one of the simplest egg dishes yet always one of the most popular with the kids.

Ingredients

4 tbsp. soft butter

4 slices fresh white bread

4 eggs

Salt and pepper

Butter both sides of bread. Using a round cookie cutter,* cut a three-inch-by-three-inch hole in each slice of bread.

Heat a large frying pan or skillet over medium-high heat. Add two to three tbsp. of butter and melt. Place a slice of bread in the pan, or more if they fit.

Now gently place a cracked egg (you can either use a whole egg or a scrambled one) into each hole in the bread; add salt and pepper. Let set for two and a half to three minutes.

With a heat-proof spatula, gently flip each slice of bread to the other side and cook for an additional thirty to forty-five seconds.

Place each Egg in a Nest on a plate and serve.

*You can also use any shape cookie cutter you prefer.

Making scrambled eggs usually turns out okay. But our aim is to make the perfect, fluffiest, creamiest scrambled eggs, and it really isn't difficult at all. In fact, once you master this easy technique, you will look forward to making the best scrambled eggs for your family and friends.

Start by melting two or more tbsp. (I like more) of butter in a large skillet or frying pan over medium heat. In medium bowl, whisk at least three eggs with two tbsp. half and half, milk, or heavy cream. (You may also use water.) Add kosher salt and pepper to taste.

Pour the egg mixture into the skillet, and lower the heat. Let the eggs set for about one minute, and then, using a heat-proof spatula, start to stir the eggs (for about three minutes; you don't have to stir them continuously in the beginning). Turn off the heat.

Now use a heat-proof spatula to slowly lift and fold the eggs for one minute longer. The eggs should be moist and shiny. That means they are done, so slide them onto a serving plate. Taste for salt and serve.

If you must, you may let the eggs linger in the pan a little longer, but remember they will continue to cook, making them firmer. When the eggs are moist but not runny, they are done, so for the perfect scrambled eggs, watch them carefully.

The more you practice this technique, the better you will get at it. It will become second nature for you to make the fluffiest, creamiest scrambled eggs.

This skillet mix is a great comfort food breakfast. For a larger group of people, just add more ingredients. Once again, you may spice it up by being creative with your choice of ingredients. Have fun and enjoy!

Ingredients

3 tbsp. butter

1 cup breakfast sausage, out of casing

1 package store-bought hash browned
   potatoes

1 onion, chopped

1 red bell pepper, diced

1 tsp. fresh thyme, chopped

1 pinch garlic powder

4 eggs

Salt and pepper

Heat butter in a large skillet or frying pan over medium-high heat. Add sausage; cook until browned, about four minutes. Add hash browns, onion, pepper, thyme, and garlic powder, mix well. Let ingredients cook undisturbed for about eight to ten minutes.

Crack your eggs in a separate bowl (check for shells). Add salt and pepper to taste. Lower heat to medium. Carefully slide eggs on to the top of the cooked sausage mixture, covering all of the sausage.

Cover the pan and let eggs cook about three minutes or until desired doneness. Once done, remove from pan and serve.

Fried Eggs and Herbed Tomatoes with Mozzarella and Basil Crème on a Crispy Crostini

This recipe may seem a little detailed, but done slowly it will be quite easy for you to do, and the results will be so rewarding. The basil cream sauce can also be used on chicken, fish, and salads. *Before you start, read the whole recipe first; then go for it.*

Ingredients

4 eggs
2 tbsp. butter
2 tomatoes, sliced ½-inch thick.
2 cups heavy cream.
3 cloves garlic, grated
½ cup crème fraiche
2 cups fresh basil, chopped
1 tbsp. crushed oregano

4 slices rustic bread
2 cups mozzarella, sliced or grated, fresh preferred
4 tbsp. Parmesan cheese, shaved
1 tsp. sugar
Kosher salt and pepper
6 tbsp. olive oil

Heat oven to 375 degrees. Place tomato slices in a baking dish and baste with two tbsp. olive oil. Add salt and pepper. Bake for five minutes.

Put crème fraiche, heavy cream, garlic, and sugar into a separate pan and simmer over low heat until reduced by a quarter, stirring occasionally. Add the chopped basil to the cream. Pour the basil cream over the tomatoes in the baking dish, and bake in the oven for another three to five minutes.

While the tomatoes are cooking, baste the bread slices lightly with some olive oil and toast under a broiler or on a stove-top grill for about one minute. After you turn the bread slices over, baste with a little more olive oil then sprinkle a little oregano and just a touch of the garlic powder on top, and then toast. Place each slice of the toasted bread on a serving plate.

Place two or three slices of tomato on each piece of bread. Then add a piece of mozzarella on top of the tomato. Place back in the oven for 3 minutes or until the cheese begins to melt.

In a heated skillet or frying pan, melt two tbsp. butter, and cook your fried eggs to your liking. Place a fried egg over the tomatoes and mozzarella cheese. Finish this amazing dish by spooning some of the basil cream sauce over the egg. Sprinkle with some shaved Parmesan cheese and serve.

Fried Eggs with Sautéed Onions and Sweet Peppers

Fried eggs with sautéed onions and sweet peppers are especially delicious because there are so many flavors that work well together. It is a colorful dish with wonderful aromas.

Ingredients

2 tbsp. olive oil

1 tbsp. garlic, minced

3 peppers, 1 red, 1 orange, 1 yellow, sliced or diced

2 large onions, sliced

1 tsp. red wine vinegar

3 to 4 tbsp. butter

6 eggs

Salt and pepper

1 tbsp. capers, chopped (optional)

Parsley for garnish

Heat frying pan over medium heat. Add olive oil, garlic, peppers, salt, and pepper and cook for three minutes. Add onions, stir occasionally, and cook for another three minutes.

Add the vinegar and cook for about two minutes. Remove from pan and set aside, keeping warm.

Wipe pan with a paper towel and add butter. When butter is melted, add eggs into pan and cook for two and a half to three minutes. (Turn over for thirty seconds for sunny side down.)

Spoon the pepper-onion mixture onto a plate. Then place eggs on top, garnish with parsley, and serve with toast.

Add capers to the onions and peppers while they cook for added taste.

Scrambled eggs can be substituted for fried eggs.

Huevos Mexicanos is similar to Huevos Rancheros but has distinct differences. The addition of home fries, jalapeno peppers, and a piece of thick Texas toast makes this a hearty and delicious breakfast.

Ingredients

6 to 8 eggs

4 tbsp. half and half

4 tbsp. butter

1 pkg. store-bought home fries

1 cup Monterey Jack cheese, shredded

1 onion, diced

Your favorite salsa, sweet or hot

Sliced jalapeno peppers (optional)

4 slices Texas toast, found in supermarket, fresh or frozen

In a bowl, whisk the eggs, half and half, salt, and pepper. Toast and butter the bread, and place each piece on a serving dish.

Heat a large skillet or frying pan over medium heat. Melt the butter. Place the onion into the hot pan and cook for two minutes. Pour the egg mixture into the skillet, and then lower the heat. Mix the cheese into the egg. Let the eggs set for about one and a half minutes. Use the spatula to lift and fold the eggs until completely cooked

As the eggs are cooking, heat the home fries in the microwave. When heated through, portion the potatoes on each slice of Texas toast.

Remove the eggs from the pan *before* they brown. Spoon some eggs over each piece of toast. Spoon some salsa on top, and jalapeno peppers to finish.

Hamburger Crumble and Fried Eggs with Hollandaise Sauce

Well-cooked hamburger simmered in butter is great as is, but combined with fried eggs, buttered rye toast, and hollandaise sauce, it is irresistibly delicious. Remember to brown the crumbled meat; it adds an extra taste level.

Ingredients

1 lb. ground chuck (80 percent lean)

4 eggs

6 tbsp. butter

1 small onion, diced

1 tsp. chopped thyme

4 slices buttered rye toast

Kosher salt and pepper

1 cup hollandaise sauce (refer to page 105)

Melt four tbsp. butter in a cast-iron skillet or nonstick frying pan over high heat. Add the chopped meat, and cook until browned. Add the onion, thyme, salt, and pepper. Remove browned meat from pan and keep warm.

Wipe the pan with a paper towel and add two tbsp. butter. When the butter is melted, crack the eggs into the pan and fry the eggs. Portion the meat on separate dishes, and place a fried egg on top. (Sunny side up eggs work great.)

Spoon some of the hollandaise sauce on top, and serve over buttered rye toast.

Huevos Rancheros

Huevos Rancheros is one of the most popular breakfast dishes. There are so many variations to this dish that you can't go wrong with the ingredients you have on hand, so mix it up and have fun.

Ingredients

Fresh tomato salsa, jarred or homemade, at room temperature
1 14-oz. can refried beans
1 chipotle chili, seeded and chopped
2 tbsp. butter
4 soft corn tortillas

1 tsp. oregano
4 fried eggs, poached if you prefer
Kosher salt and fresh pepper
1 avocado, pitted, peeled, and thinly sliced
1/2 cup Monterey Jack cheese, grated

Wrap the tortillas in a dry napkin and place in a microwave for about ten seconds; then place each tortilla on a separate plate.

In a small saucepan, warm the beans and chilies. Spread a quarter of the bean mixture over each tortilla.

Fry the eggs in the butter, and place one egg on top of the beans on each tortilla.

Spread desired amount of salsa over each egg, and add salt, pepper, and oregano to taste. Add a slice of the avocado, and sprinkle a liberal amount of the Jack cheese on top and serve.

Steak and eggs may be the heartiest of all breakfasts. Some advocate using a thick steak, but I differ for a few reasons. First, a too thick a steak costs much more. It takes longer to cook, which means it is harder to coordinate with the rest of the breakfast, and it is harder to judge just when it is done. You can do whatever is best for your taste, but I recommend a steak no more than one inch thick. Use as many steaks and eggs as you need. You may even slice the steak to make more servings.

Ingredients

1 sirloin steak
2 tbsp. butter
2 tbsp. vegetable or olive oil
½ tsp. lemon juice
1 tsp. Worcestershire sauce

1 tsp. Lawry's seasoned salt, found in the spice aisle of the supermarket
Salt and pepper
2 eggs
1 tsp. parsley, finely chopped for garnish

Mix lemon juice, Worcestershire sauce, and oil in a bowl, and then pour into a plastic bag or Pyrex dish. Place steak in bag or dish. Let it marinate for up to an hour.

Preheat a cast iron skillet or frying pan over medium heat, and then add butter to melt. Remove the steak from the marinade and pat dry.

Sprinkle salt, pepper, and Lawry's onto both sides of steak. Raise heat to high, and place steak into the skillet to cook for three to four minutes per side or to your liking. Steaks need to "rest" when finished cooking so the juices redistribute throughout the whole steak (remove the steak when done and let it rest on a plate for about five minutes while you cook the eggs).

Now cook your eggs as you normally would. Fried or scrambled eggs are best for this dish.

Transfer the rested steak to a dish, and place the eggs alongside or on top of the steak.

Sprinkle parsley over the finished dish, and enjoy an amazing breakfast.

Hula Eggs are fun to make. While you are preparing this Hawaiian breakfast dish, you will notice that the smell of the caramelized pineapple is so amazing that you will feel you are in Hawaii. The unusual taste of the pineapple, ham, onion, and eggs is wonderful. It is really fun to play some Hawaiian music while enjoying this so *'ono'* (delicious) breakfast. After you make this tasty dish the kids will say, "Hana hou"! (Do it again!)

Ingredients

4 tbsp. butter

2 eggs

¼ cup ham, diced

½ cup onion, diced

1 slice of pineapple, roughly ½ inch thickness. Canned pineapple is also okay

Salt and pepper

In a medium-hot frying pan, add one tbsp. butter. As butter begins to melt, add pineapple. (You want the pineapple to caramelize, so sauté in butter for two minutes; then turn over and cook for one minute.) Remove from heat and set aside.

In the same pan, add one tbsp. butter and diced onion and sauté for three to four minutes or until translucent. Add diced ham to the onions and cook for two minutes more. Remove from heat and set aside (keep warm).

Lower heat, and wipe pan with paper towel. Add remaining two tbsp. butter. When butter is melted, add eggs and fry to desired doneness.

To serve, place warm pineapple on a plate and slide fried eggs on top of the pineapple. Spoon sautéed onions and ham on top. Serve.

Your family will say "Mahalo nui loa!" (Thank you very much!)

Serves one.

If you had to pick one breakfast or brunch dish that is both delicious and impressive, it would definitely be *Tuscan eggs*. It looks, smells, and tastes amazing. It is as exciting to make as it is exciting to present to your family or guests—and is actually quite easy to make.

Ingredients

4 slices rustic bread or Panini bread

6 slices prosciutto

8 tbsp. extra virgin olive oil

2 tsp. fresh oregano, minced, dry oregano is also okay

2 cloves garlic, finely minced

4 eggs

Kosher salt and ground black pepper

Parmigiano reggiano cheese, shaved

Fresh basil for garnish, optional

Heat oil and garlic in a small pan, about two to three minutes.

Place bread slices on parchment-lined baking sheet. When the oil and garlic are finished heating, brush both sides of bread with the garlic and oil mix. Heat your oven broiler to medium-high, and slide baking sheet onto middle rack. Broil bread until lightly toasted on both sides, watching so it doesn't burn.

Place the prosciutto on a lined baking sheet. Broil prosciutto until it's slightly crisp. Remove from broiler. Put prosciutto on a separate dish and with your hands, gently crumble the prosciutto into one- to two-inch pieces.

Pour remaining oil into a small bowl and add oregano. Add two tbsp. of your garlic herb oil mix into a large heated frying pan. Crack eggs and place them gently into pan. Sprinkle with salt and pepper, and then lower heat. As eggs cook, spoon oil mix over the top, allowing the eggs to cook for three minutes, and then remove from pan.

Place one egg on each piece of bread. Sprinkle liberally with crumbled prosciutto.

To finish, spoon more oil mix on top of eggs and then shave a few slices of the Parmigiano on top.

Garnish with some basil and serve.

If you like salmon, you will love it combined with the fluffiest scrambled eggs. For a little added flavor you may add a dash of Old Bay* seasoning to the mix as it cooks.

Ingredients

2 tsp. corn oil

1 small onion, diced

8 eggs

3 tbsp. milk or half and half

2 tbsp. butter

½ lb. smoked salmon, sliced into half-inch strips

2 oz. cream cheese, cubed

1½ tbsp. chives, chopped

4 slices rustic bread, toasted, or English muffins

Heat oil in a frying pan over medium heat. Add onion with salt and pepper and cook for five to six minutes (until translucent).

Whisk eggs with the half and half or milk in a bowl and add salt and pepper. Add the two tbsp. of butter to the onions. Lower the heat. Add eggs to pan and let them set for about one and a half minutes, and then mix with a coated whisk or heat-proof spatula.

Now add the salmon strips while still moving the eggs. Continue to cook the eggs for another minute. Add cream cheese to the mixture, and stir to melt. Using a heat-proof spatula, gently lift and fold eggs to allow the eggs to cook. Turn off the heat; the eggs should be shiny and moist.

Toast your English muffins or bread and place on a serving dish, and spoon the eggs and salmon over the toast, adding salt and pepper to taste. Sprinkle with chives and serve.

*Old Bay seasoning can be found in the spice aisle of your grocer.

Omelets

Making the perfect omelet is much easier than it looks. The funny thing is it really doesn't have to be perfect to be good. Just follow the instructions below, go slow, and "get 'er done". If it isn't quite perfect, don't worry; practice makes perfect. Remember, doing it together is the important thing, and make it fun. Let your family pick the ingredients for their own omelets. You can also make one or two big omelets for a crowd.

Ingredients (for one omelet)

3 extra-large or jumbo eggs   2 tbsp. half and half

Kosher salt and pepper   2 tbsp. butter

In a bowl, whisk together the first three ingredients. Whisk them well because a little air in the mixture will make a nice, fluffy omelet. You can even use a hand blender if you choose.

Heat a skillet or frying pan over medium heat, and then add the butter to melt. (I usually add a bit more butter; I just can't resist it.)

Pour the egg mixture into the pan. As the eggs begin to set, lower the heat (this should be about two minutes). Using a heat-proof spatula, begin to lift the omelet from the sides to let the uncooked liquid flow underneath to the bottom of the pan. Continue this process until there is no longer any runny liquid on top—about another minute.

Now would be the time to add your cheese or other items (i.e., vegetables, bacon, ham, etc.). Gently fold over one side of the omelet to the other. Turn off the heat, and cook for about another thirty seconds.

Tilt the pan and slide out the omelet, gently folding it in half onto a serving plate.

Watch the omelet as you go, and try not to burn or brown the bottom, so watch the heat.

If you need help folding the omelet from one side to the other, lift one side of the pan to help with the fold.

If you are using meats, onions, peppers, or other veggies, you may want to sauté them in a little butter before you add them to the omelet or as you are starting to cook the omelet. The usual rule should be to cook cold cuts (like salami) for about one to two minutes. Veggies, on the other hand, should cook for about two to four minutes, depending on your preference.

The omelet bar is a great and fun way to get the whole family or guests involved in making breakfast together. The kids may choose exactly what they would like to have in their omelets. The omelet bar is a good step toward teaching children about nutrition and how to cook foods that are healthy. The choices for the omelet bar are virtually endless; here are several options to get you started.

Ingredients

Meats
Ham, bacon, Canadian bacon, chorizo, sopressata, salami, steak, corned beef hash, prosciutto.

Veggies
Tomatoes, sliced zucchini, arugula, spinach, onions, scallions, mushrooms, asparagus, broccoli, chilies, home fried potatoes, shallots, olives, hot and sweet peppers, jalapeno peppers, avocado.

Cheeses
Swiss, gouda, mozzarella, Monterey Jack, cream cheese, cheddar, feta, parmesan, blue cheese, asiago, goat cheese

Herbs
Chives, oregano, basil, dill, parsley, cilantro, minced garlic

Fruits
Assorted fruits

Accompaniments
Assorted breads, bagels, butter, jams, jellies, grits, or salsa

Okay, now it's your turn. Have fun adding to the list, and then *"just belly up to the bar"*, *"—the omelet bar"*, that is!

This omelet is very thin and light, so use your largest frying pan to spread out the eggs

Ingredients

8 eggs	1 tbsp. thyme, minced
1tbsp. basil, minced	3 tbsp. half and half
1 tbsp. chives, minced	Salt and fresh pepper
1 tbsp. parsley, minced	4 tbsp. butter

Whisk together all ingredients except butter. Melt the butter in a large nonstick skillet or frying pan over medium-high heat. Do not burn the butter.

Pour egg mixture into pan. Let eggs set, one to two minutes. Scrape eggs from side of pan by sliding a spatula completely around the inside of the skillet. Now start to lift the edges of the setting eggs. This will enable the uncooked liquid to flow to bottom of the pan.

Once the bottom is completely set, place a wide spatula under one-quarter of the omelet and gently fold over to the center. Do the same with the other side. If you have any difficulty doing this, just fold the omelet in half.

Slide the finished omelet onto a dish and garnish.

It is easy to see the rainbow in this colorful omelet. It is also very versatile because you can substitute several ingredients to spice it up or smooth it out. Either way you will feel like you found a pot of gold after you finish.

Ingredients

8 eggs

½ cup ham, diced

¾ cup cheddar cheese; you may substitute Monterey Jack cheese

¼ cup each, red, yellow, and orange peppers, finely diced

1 red onion, finely diced

Hot peppers, finely diced, optional, such as jalapenos or chilies

4 tbsp. butter

4 tbsp. half and half or milk

1 tsp. Italian parsley, finely diced

Chopped chives for garnish

Combine eggs, half and half, salt, and pepper in a large bowl and whisk well. Add ham, cheese, parsley, hot peppers, and onions and mix well.

Melt butter in a large skillet or frying pan over medium heat. Add the egg mixture and lower the heat. Let set for one and a half minutes. Lift and fold eggs with a heat-proof spatula, scraping the sides to let uncooked liquid to flow to the bottom.

When all the liquid is set (three to four minutes), use a large plate to help flip the omelet over. Cook for one more minute.

Slide the omelet onto a serving dish. Garnish with chives, serve, and then watch the rainbow of smiles on your family's faces.

This is an interesting omelet. You may want to order it in Down East Maine to the Massachusetts coast or even Montauk, New York. You don't have to be a seafood lover to enjoy it. If you are not fond of clams, you may substitute oysters or mussels.

Ingredients

4 eggs

4 tbsp. butter

1 tbsp. vegetable oil

1/2 cup heavy cream or half and half

1/2 cup little neck clams, chopped and drained

Kosher salt and black pepper to taste

½ tsp. Old Bay seasoning, optional

1 tbsp. fresh thyme, chopped

Heat a cast iron skillet or frying pan over medium-high heat. Add two tbsp. butter and oil to the pan. Whisk the eggs, heavy cream, salt, and pepper.

Add the chopped clams to the oil and melted butter. Sprinkle the Old Bay seasoning over the clams and stir. Cook the clams for about one minute (to your desired texture), stirring occasionally.

Place the remaining two tbsp. of butter into the pan with cooked clams. Add the egg mixture to the skillet. Once the eggs are set, lift and fold the edges, letting the uncooked liquid flow to the bottom of the omelet.

Once the omelet is done, gently fold one side over the other. Or if you prefer, you may place the skillet in a 375-degree oven (oven-proof skillet) for about one to two minutes until golden brown. When cooked, slide onto a serving dish and serve.

A little hot sauce, or a lot, goes great with this omelet.

Hawaiian Omelet with Pineapple, Coconut-Rum Aloha Sauce

Like most omelets, the Hawaiian omelet is quite easy to make and is so "ono" (delicious). The Aloha sauce is even easier to prepare. When you make the Aloha sauce, you can use light rum if you don't have any coconut rum. For the kids, just eliminate the rum altogether; it will still taste great. When you make this omelet, the fragrances of the Hawaiian Islands will just captivate you. Your family and guests will just love it and say, *"E' ai Ka Kou"*—(Let's eat!)

Omelet Ingredients

6 eggs

6 strips bacon, cooked and crumbled

2 fairly large shallots, diced

½ cup red bell pepper, diced

½ cup Swiss cheese, grated

4 tbsp. butter

2 tbsp. half and half or milk

2 tbsp. crème of coconut; you may sub ½ tsp. coconut extract

1 tsp. thyme

Salt and pepper

Aloha Sauce Ingredients

1 8-oz. can crushed pineapple, drained

1 tbsp. coconut rum; you may substitute 1 tsp. coconut extract to replace rum

1 tbsp. crème of coconut or 1 tsp. coconut extract

2 tbsp. brown sugar

Heat all sauce ingredients in small saucepan then serve over Hawaiian omelet.

Melt butter in a medium-size cast iron skillet or frying pan (about ten inches). Put shallots in skillet and sauté for about three minutes. Add peppers, and cook for two more minutes. Add the bacon.

Whisk together eggs, milk, crème of coconut, salt, and pepper. Then add grated cheese. Pour egg and cheese mixture into pan with shallots and peppers. Let eggs set for about two minutes.

Lift the sides to let uncooked egg slide to the bottom of pan. Continue until all of the egg is set. With a wide spatula, gently flip the omelet to the other side, and cook for one more minute.

Slide omelet from pan to a serving plate. Top with Aloha sauce. Now everyone shouts, in true Hawaiian fashion—"A*ahh-looo-ha*!"

Herbed Italian Spinach Omelet with Parmesan and Swiss Cheese

This very special omelet emits the amazing tastes and aromas of a quaint Italian hosteria, tucked into a side street of Tuscany. It is such a hearty breakfast dish and could even be served for brunch or a light dinner.

Ingredients

1 lb. fresh spinach, chopped

1/4 cup parsley, chopped

6 to 8 eggs

3 cloves garlic, minced

2 small onions, chopped

1/2 cup Parmesan cheese, grated

1 cup Swiss cheese, grated

3 tbsp. butter

3 tbsp. unflavored breadcrumbs

3 tbsp. extra virgin olive oil

Kosher salt and pepper

Over medium heat, add butter and one tbsp. oil to a large cast iron skillet or frying pan. Add garlic and onion to pan and sauté for about four minutes or until onion becomes translucent. Add the spinach, parsley, salt, and pepper. Cook until spinach is wilted.

In a large bowl, whisk the eggs. Add in the cheeses and breadcrumbs and whisk gently.

Add remaining oil to the spinach mix and then add egg and cheese mixture to the skillet. Let the bottom set firmly, and then lift with a spatula to let uncooked liquid flow to the bottom of the pan.

Place a large dish on top of omelet pan to aid you in turning the omelet over, and then slide it back into the skillet to cook the other side for three minutes. It is a tricky move, but you can do it if you go slowly.

Remove from pan by sliding omelet onto a serving dish, divide, and serve. *Buon giorno* and *Bouna Festa*.

The Topkapi Palace was built during the Ottoman Empire in fifteenth-century Turkey. It was famous for its magnificent kitchens that were contained in fifteen domed buildings. Thousands of great meals were prepared there using great sauces with a Mediterranean flair, similar to the Topkapi sauce below. Incidentally, a great and exciting movie about the Topkapi diamond was filmed there in 1964. It is sometimes funny but also a nail-biting thriller. This sauce is great and can be used on many other dishes

Omelet Ingredients

4 to 6 eggs

1 slice fresh mozzarella, quarter-inch thick by about four inches round

4 tsp. olive oil

Pinch of red pepper flakes

½ tsp. oregano

2 tbsp. milk or half and half

Salt and pepper

Topkapi Sauce Ingredients

2 tbsp. olive oil

1 cup crushed tomatoes

1/2 cup shallots, minced

2 cloves garlic, minced

1 tbsp. capers, chopped

1 tsp. Italian parsley, chopped

1 tsp. oregano

1 tsp. fresh thyme

½ tsp. onion powder

Salt and pepper

Heat a saucepan over medium heat. Add oil and warm. Add garlic and shallots and sauté for four to five minutes. Lower heat and add remaining ingredients and cook for about twelve minutes. Pour over omelet.

Heat a medium-sized skillet or frying pan on medium heat. Add two tsp. of the oil into the pan and heat for thirty seconds to a minute.

Using tongs put the piece of mozzarella into the hot oil. After one minute, turn the cheese over. Season with salt, pepper, oregano, and red pepper flakes. Cook for one minute more, and then remove cheese from pan and set aside.

Combine eggs, milk, salt, and pepper in a bowl. In same frying pan that you cooked the cheese in, add two more tsp. of oil. The pan should still be hot, so you can put your eggs in after at least thirty seconds of warming the oil.

Let the eggs set (about one and a half minutes), and then start to lift the edges to let the liquid flow to bottom of pan. Gently flip the omelet to the other side. Place the finished piece of mozzarella cheese on top of the omelet. Gently fold each side of the omelet toward the middle to cover the cheese, like a neat package. Slide onto a serving dish, top with the Topkapi sauce, and serve.

This is an omelet that is near and very dear to this dad's heart. Not only is it so delicious, but for our family, it has so many memories. Our boys used to love to help chop up the ingredients and help cook the omelet. As time moved along and they went to college, they would come home after a fun night and raid the fridge for a post-midnight snack of our pre-chopped meats and veggies readied for tomorrow morning's omelets. We will see what happens when their kids grow up. Keep tuned!

Ingredients

8 to 10 eggs

4 tbsp. butter

4 tbsp. half and half

1 onion, chopped

1 bell pepper, diced

½ cup Genoa salami, sliced into strips or small dice

½ cup ham, chopped into small dice

½ cup Swiss cheese, sliced into strips

Salt and pepper

1 tbsp. fresh parsley, minced

Preheat oven to 375 degrees. Heat a large skillet or heat-proof frying pan over medium heat. Melt the butter in the heated pan. Add the onion and pepper, and sauté for two minutes. Add salami and ham and cook for one to two minutes more.

Whisk the eggs, half and half, salt, and pepper in a bowl, and then pour into the pan with the other ingredients. Let the eggs set, scraping the sides gently. As the bottom starts to set, lift the sides of omelet with a heat-proof spatula to let the uncooked liquid to flow to bottom of the pan, and then place cheese on top.

Using an oven mitt put the skillet into the heated oven until the cheese starts to melt. Remove from oven, and slide the omelet onto a serving plate. Sprinkle with parsley and serve.

Recipe for Steak & Eggs on page 21

Shore Dinner Omelet with Lemon White Wine Butter Cream Sauce

This omelet is a favorite at the shore. For those who love seafood or love to go to the beach or shore destinations, the tastes in this omelet brings you right back to those favorite spots. At first glance, this omelet may look a little complicated, but it is just an omelet with a sauce. Once again, go slow, think it out, and then start. It is delicious with or without the sauce. For the kids, just delete the wine. You can choose any variation of seafood. Below is a sample for you to try.

Omelet Ingredients

6 eggs

2 tbsp. half and half

4 oz. shrimp, chopped

4 oz. lobster, chopped

1 scallion, finely chopped

1 tsp. Old Bay seasoning,(in the spice aisle of most grocery stores)

¼ tsp. dill

3 tbsp. olive oil

2 tbsp. butter

2 dashes Tabasco sauce, optional

1 tbsp. parsley, chopped, for garnish

Salt and pepper

Butter Cream Sauce Ingredients

6 tbsp. butter

2 tbsp. all-purpose flour

4 tbsp. dry white wine

3 tsp. lemon juice.

1/3 cup heavy cream

1 tbsp. Dijon mustard

1 egg yolk

½ small onion, finely chopped.

¼ cup parmesan cheese, shredded

1 tsp. dry tarragon

1 tbsp. lemon zest

Salt and pepper

NOTE: You may want to make the sauce first, to make it a little easier. When the sauce is finished, just remove it from the heat and keep warm, or just microwave it for a minute or so before serving.

In a large bowl, mix the seafood, one tsp. of the olive oil, scallion, Old Bay seasoning, dill, Tabasco (if using), and salt and pepper. Let marinate for about thirty minutes.

In a large skillet or frying pan, heat two tsp. of the olive oil and then sauté the seafood mix for about three minutes or until translucent. Remove from heat and set aside.

In another bowl, whisk the eggs, half and half, salt, and pepper.

Melt two tbsp. butter in a skillet or frying pan over medium heat. When melted, lower the heat and add the egg mix. Let the eggs set for about two to three minutes, lifting and folding as you normally would.

Once the eggs set, gently flip the omelet to the other side and cook for one more minute. Add the seafood mix onto one side of the omelet, and gently fold over the other side. Remove and set aside.

To Make the Butter Cream Sauce

Wipe out your skillet, and melt the butter. Add the flour, stirring as you go. Slowly pour in the cream, lemon zest, lemon juice, onion, wine, Dijon mustard, egg yolk, tarragon, salt, and pepper.

Cook over medium heat for about five minutes, stirring occasionally. Finally, add the cheese, and let it melt for one minute more.

To serve, portion the omelet onto separate plates. Spoon some sauce over each serving. Sprinkle some parsley over each serving and enjoy.

Pancakes, Waffles, Ebelskievers, and Crepes

Incredible Crepes with Warm Very Berry Maple Sauce

When making crepes, you have two choices. You can make the batter from scratch or purchase a prepared crepe mix and just add the wet ingredients. To start it might be easier to use the crepe mix. Either way you will be in for a treat.

A crepe pan is good to have but not necessary; an eight-inch nonstick frying pan works fine. A Teflon-coated pair of tongs or an offset spatula helps to flip the crepes.

Ingredients

1 cup all-purpose flour

½ tsp. kosher salt

1 egg

1¼ cups milk

2 tbsp. butter, melted and cooled

Start by putting the flour and salt into a large bowl. Make a well in the middle. Crack the egg, and place it in the well. Slowly add the milk, whisking the mixture gently as you go. Then add the cooled, melted butter and whisk. You want the batter to be smooth and fairly thin, but don't over-whisk.

Heat a nonstick pan over medium heat. Melt one tbsp. butter in the pan and then pour three tbsp. of the batter into the pan (swirl to thinly coat). Cook the crepe for about one minute, and then gently flip to the other side for about one minute more.

Continue process with remaining batter. Keep the crepes warm by stacking them and placing a warm, damp, soft cloth on top or by putting the completed crepes in a warm 200-degree oven.

As you progress in crepe making, you can flip the crepes by lifting them with a fork and carefully turning them with your fingers. Be very careful not to burn your fingertips.

Warm very berry maple sauce recipe found in "Tops in Toppings."

Recipe for Potato Pancakes on page 86

The first-time our family had challah bread French toast was at Disney World many years ago. Everyone loved it. Chip and Dale stopped by our table to make sure, "We ate it all up." We chose to top our French toast with a mixture of cinnamon and sugar and topped that with warm maple syrup and melted butter. It was soooo good. If you choose, you can have your French toast with whipped cream and fruit or just about anything you like.

Ingredients

6 eggs

1½ cups heavy cream or half and half

1 tsp. vanilla extract

1 tbsp. maple syrup, honey, or both.

1 tsp. cinnamon

4 tbsp. butter

Kosher salt

1 loaf challah bread, sliced into one-inch-thick slices

1 cup warmed maple syrup, more if needed

Whisk together the eggs, half and half, vanilla, one tbsp. of the maple syrup, cinnamon, and salt. Dip each slice of bread in the egg mixture, soaking each side well.

Melt two tbsp. butter in a large skillet over medium heat. Place a slice of bread (or more) in the skillet and cook for about three minutes or until golden brown on both sides.

As you fry the remaining pieces, add butter as needed. Remove from skillet and keep warm until ready to serve.

Serve with warm maple syrup and softened butter. A sprinkle of confectioners' sugar looks great and tastes even better

For the topping that our family had at Disney World, mix one cup sugar with two to three tsp. cinnamon and sprinkle over the French toast. Top with warm syrup and melted butter.

Aside from tasting so good and looking great, ebelskivers are just plain fun to make.

You can have them for breakfast or lunch, and they are perfect for brunch. You only need to purchase an ebelskiver pan, sold just about everywhere now. Once you do, the rest becomes easy. You may use the ebelskiver batter recipe on page 50, purchase ebelskiver batter mix, or simply use pancake batter.

Ebelskivers can be eaten plain or with jam, jelly fillings, sweets, meats, or cheeses. Kids love to help fill the ebelskivers and to roll them as they cook. The technique is easy.

Heat the ebelskiver pan over medium heat. Butter or spray the wells of the pan so the batter won't stick.

Fill each well with batter about 1/3 full. Next add your fillings if using. Then add a little more batter almost to the top of each well.

Cook the first side for about four minutes. Then, using a fork or chopstick, gently roll the skiver over to the other side. (Small bubbles will indicate that the skiver is ready to flip.) Cook the other side for two to three minutes more.

The finished skivers should be golden in color. When cooked to your liking remove each ebelskiver to a cookie tray and place in a heated oven at about 200 degrees to keep warm.

There are many variations to ebelskiver batter. This recipe is very simple and seems to work the best.

Ingredients

1 cup all-purpose flour.
2 tsp. sugar
½ tsp. baking powder
½ tsp. salt

2 large eggs
1 cup whole milk
3 tbsp. unsalted butter, melted and cooled

In a large bowl sift together the flour, sugar, baking powder, and salt. In a separate bowl whisk the eggs, milk, and melted butter. Add the egg and milk mixture to the flour mix, and whisk gently. Don't worry if the batter is a bit lumpy.

To add flavor to the batter, you may add ¾ tsp. vanilla extract to the mixture.

When you taste these fluffy apple-filled skivers, your senses will be transported to a warm and cozy country inn with the smells and flavors of a very special breakfast. These ebelskivers are also great for brunch, dessert, or snacking. Use your favorite ebelskiver batter or the batter recipe on page 50. Follow directions on page 48 to cook your Skivers.

Ingredients for filling

¼–½ cup unsalted butter

2 tbsp. sugar

2 tbsp. brown sugar.

¼ tsp. cinnamon

Pinch of grated nutmeg

Pinch allspice

¼ tsp. salt

2 Granny Smith apples, peeled and diced

Melt butter in saucepan. Add the rest of the ingredients. Cook over medium heat until apples are tender. Cool slightly.

Don't overfill the ebelskivers. When finished you may top each skiver with some maple sugar, confectioners' sugar, or some of the apple pie filling

Should make about fifteen skivers.

Now that you are comfortable with making these delicious, fun-to-make skivers, here are some great fillings and toppings to use.

Jams, jellies, and fruit curds

Whipped cream

Cheese filling

Cheese

Chocolate and chocolate syrup

Carmel and butterscotch sauce

Cinnamon

Confectioner's sugar

Cream cheese

Maple syrup

Bacon bits

Ham, salami bits, etc.

Salsas

You can use your imagination and have lots of family fun creating these fabulous treats.

Griddlecakes with Canadian Bacon and Maple Sugar Rum Apples

If you like griddle cakes, you will love this recipe. Use my recipe for the best buttermilk pancakes to start. Add the Canadian bacon, and then smother them with the wonderful maple sugar rum apples. You can skip the rum if you wish (there is plenty of flavor without the rum). You can also make two batches of apples, one with rum and one without. You decide.

Ingredients

Buttermilk pancake recipe (page 54)
4 tbsp. butter
½ cup dark brown sugar
¼ cup maple syrup
3 tbsp. rum

1 tsp. cinnamon
1 lb. Canadian bacon, sliced
1 red apple, peeled and sliced fairly thin
1 green apple, peeled and sliced fairly thin

Make griddle cakes (pancakes) as you normally would, and then set aside and keep warm

In a bowl, combine the brown sugar and cinnamon.

In a large skillet or frying pan, melt two tbsp. of the butter. Lower the heat, and then add the sugar mixture and whisk into the melted butter. Add the maple syrup right away, and blend for about one minute. Make sure the sugar is completely dissolved.

Remove the pan from the heat and add the rum (if using). Put the pan back on the heat, and carefully add the apples to the mixture. Cook over moderate heat for about seven to eight minutes. Keep an eye on the pan, stirring occasionally. Remove the apples from the pan and keep warm.

Melt the remaining two tbsp. of the butter in the same pan used for the apples. Add the Canadian bacon to the pan and cook for about three to four minutes.

Place the griddle cakes on a serving plate, and then add the Canadian bacon. Finally, spoon the maple sugar rum apples over the top and serve.

The steaming griddle cakes and hot sauce make an irresistibly delicious breakfast dish

You may also use the apple mixture over ice cream, fruit, waffles, or anything you wish for a tasty treat for your family or friends.

I think buttermilk pancakes are without a doubt the best! There is so much richness and flavor that each bite keeps you wanting more.

Ingredients

1 3/4 cups buttermilk

2 cups all-purpose flour

3 eggs

1 tbsp. fine sugar

1 tbsp. baking powder

1 tsp. baking soda

4 tbsp. unsalted butter, melted and cooled

2 tbs. butter or spray to grease the griddle

Mix or whisk the buttermilk, eggs, and melted and cooled butter. In a large bowl, whisk together the flour, sugar, baking powder, and baking soda. Add the buttermilk mixture to the dry ingredients, and mix well. Heat a nonstick griddle over medium heat. Butter or spray the griddle.

Spoon or pour batter onto griddle. Cook until bubbles start to form on top of pancakes. Turn the pancakes over with a heat-proof spatula, and cook until lightly browned.

As you finish cooking the pancakes, stack them and keep warm in a 200-

degree oven.

A nice addition is to serve your pancakes with bacon or sausage.

Toppings are limitless, from butter and maple syrup to ice cream and whipped cream. Make it fun with cookie cutter shapes and designs made with bacon strips and syrups. The kids will love it.

Last note on buttermilk pancakes; of course you may use a buttermilk pancake mix. Our favorite is King Arthur Buttermilk Pancake Mix. You will get great results even if you use a prepared mix.

Making the best pancakes takes just a little care, but the results are worth it. These pancakes are just amazing. You will marvel at the taste. A stack of the *best pancakes* with butter and warm maple syrup is the ultimate breakfast dish.

Ingredients

1 1/2 cups all-purpose flour

2 tsp. baking powder

¼ tsp. baking soda

1 tsp. salt

3 tbsp. confectioners' sugar

2 eggs

2 tsp. melted butter

1 cup milk or buttermilk (add more if you need it)

3 tbsp. Vermont maple syrup

1 tbsp. vanilla extract

4 tbsp. unsalted butter, melted, plus more to grease skillet

Combine flour, baking powder, baking soda, and salt into a bowl. Sift together and mix.

In another bowl, whisk together eggs, milk, confectioners' sugar, melted butter, maple syrup, and vanilla. Add them to the bowl of sifted flour mix and either beat or whisk. The mixture, which is now your pancake batter, can be mildly lumpy.

Heat a large nonstick skillet or frying pan over medium heat. When heated, melt two tbsp. butter to grease the pan.

Pour about four tbsp. of batter (you can just eyeball it) onto the pan for each pancake and cook until bubbles start to form. With a heat-proof spatula, gently turn the pancakes over and cook the other side until lightly browned.

Remove from pan and keep warm. Serve with melted butter and heated maple syrup or your favorite topping.

Now those are the *BEST PANCAKES*.

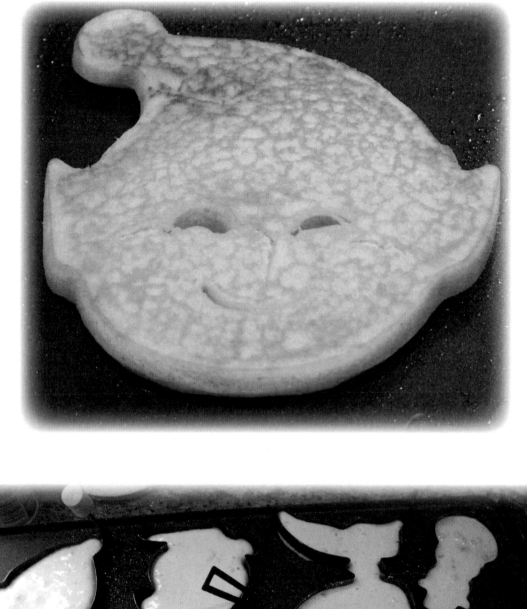

The kids just love raisin swirl French toast. There is something about the taste that they just keep wanting more. If your children don't care for raisins, just buy the cinnamon swirl bread without the raisins. Your family will want to help you make the egg mixture, and they just love to dip the bread in it.

Ingredients

4 slices store-bought raisin swirl bread

4 eggs

1 cup half and half or milk

1 tbsp. sugar

1 tsp. cinnamon

½ tsp. vanilla extract

½ cup unsalted butter

Pinch of ground nutmeg

Pinch of salt

In a large bowl, combine eggs, half and half or milk, sugar, cinnamon, nutmeg (if using), vanilla, and salt. Melt two tbsp. butter over medium heat in a large preheated skillet.

Dip each slice of bread in the egg mixture, coating well. As butter starts to foam, add pieces of bread to the pan. Cook each piece for about two to three minutes per side or until golden brown. Add more butter as necessary to cook remaining bread, and then remove to serving platter.

Toppings may include:

- Butter
- Maple syrup
- Jelly
- Whipped cream
- Assorted fruits
- Powdered or granulated sugar
- Cinnamon

Ham and Bananas Foster Waffles

This breakfast dish is a particular treat that can also be used for brunch or even," breakfast for dinner".

For brunch, you can add some Crème de Banana or rum. Making the dish this way, if you choose to add rum, is safer with no flambéing. Remember, you don't need alcohol to make this breakfast dish great.

Ingredients

5 tbsp. unsalted butter

1 cup light brown sugar

½ tsp. cinnamon

2 ripe bananas, peeled, sliced in half, and then cut into chunks

¼ cup light rum or Crème de Banana liqueur

4 slices smoked ham, about 1/4 inch thick

Waffle recipe below, or good-quality frozen waffles,

Make your waffles and keep warm in a pre-heated oven set to 200 degrees.

In a large skillet or frying pan, melt one tbsp. butter; add the ham and brown, turning once. Remove the ham and set aside and cover to keep warm.

Wipe the skillet with a paper towel; add the remaining four tbsp. of butter. When butter is melted, add the sugar, cinnamon, and rum or Crème de Banana. Cook for two minutes, and then add the sliced banana. Simmer for three minutes while gently stirring.

To serve, place a warm waffle on a plate. Then add a slice of ham, some bananas, and syrup on top of each waffle and enjoy the amazing flavors.

Waffle Ingredients

1 egg, room temperature and separated

1 cup all-purpose flour

1 tsp. baking powder

1/8 tsp. salt

1 tbsp. sugar

¾ cup milk

4 tbsp. butter, melted and cooled.

Beat egg white until stiff peaks form, and then set aside. Mix all dry ingredients together and set aside. Combine egg yolk, milk, and butter, and then add to the dry ingredients, mixing until just blended. Fold in egg white until mixed. Don't overbeat.

Waffles (recipe on page 59)

Heat your waffle maker.

Pour quarter cup of batter into buttered (or sprayed) waffle maker. Don't overfill, and cook till golden brown.

Caramelized Bananas Ingredients

4 oz. butter, cubed

3 tbsp. dark corn syrup

3 bananas, peeled and sliced

Caramelized Bananas

Melt cubed butter with corn syrup in a saucepan over low heat.

Simmer for several minutes until mixture begins to thicken. Add sliced bananas to mixture. Gently stir to coat bananas and cook for two minutes.

Pour over completed waffles.

You may also use the banana mix on pancakes.

Breakfast Sandwiches and Paninis

Croque Madame is a fancy name for a great breakfast sandwich. The recipe is easy to follow, incredibly delicious, and fun to make. You can certainly use the sauce on other breakfast dishes.

Read the recipe first, and then just go step by step.

Ingredients

For the Béchamel Sauce *(you can make ahead, refrigerate, and warm up before use)*

2 tbsp. butter, softened	4 eggs
2 tbsp. flour	8 slices crusty bread
2 tsp. dry mustard	1 tbsp. Dijon mustard
1 cup whole milk	8 slices smoked ham
Salt and pepper	1 ½ cup gruyere cheese, shredded
For the Sandwich	

This is fun and easy, so let's get going.

In a saucepan over moderate heat, melt two tbsp. softened butter. Add the flour and dry mustard, stirring and watching that it doesn't burn (about two minutes). Lower the heat and add the milk, stirring constantly. The mixture will start to thicken. When the mixture comes to a boil, cook for two to three more minutes. Add salt and pepper to taste, stir, and then remove from heat.

Butter one side of each of four slices of the bread, turn the bread over, and spread some mustard on the other side. Heat a large skillet or frying pan over medium heat, and then add the four slices of buttered bread, side by side (buttered side *down*).

With a large spoon, spread some Béchamel sauce over the mustard on top of each slice of bread.

Now add enough Gruyere cheese to cover the sauce.

Next, add 2 slices of the ham to each slice of bread. Add a touch more sauce on top of the ham.

Now, butter the remaining 4 slices of bread and cover the sandwiches in the pan, and then flip the sandwich over so the newly buttered side is *down*. Cook until the cheese is melted and both sides are nicely browned (about three to four minutes).

While the sandwiches are finishing, heat a large frying pan and melt two to three tbsp. butter. Add four cracked eggs. Add salt and pepper, and cook to your individual taste.

Place each sandwich on a separate plate, and add an egg on top of each. With a spoon, add some sauce on top of each completed sandwich.

You did great! From start to finish, this sandwich should take about twenty-five minutes.

La Jolla, California is one of the most beautiful cities in the world. It has incredible beaches, views, and shopping and great restaurants to match. This recipe brings back great memories of a fabulous breakfast our family enjoyed while visiting this beautiful city.

Ingredients

2 eggs (for fried eggs), (3 for scrambled)

2 tbsp. butter (for cooking eggs)

6 strips bacon

4 slices bread of your choice

4 slices Brie cheese

8 slices avocado (4 slices for sandwiches, 4 slices for garnish)

1 jar mango or peach chutney

2 tbsp. Dijon mustard

2 more tbsp. softened butter for bread

Salt and pepper

Kettle potato chips (optional)

Cook the bacon, but don't make it too crisp.

Scramble or fry the eggs (your choice).

Lightly butter one side of the bread. Place two slices of cheese on each of the two slices of the bread. Spread the Dijon mustard on the remaining two slices of bread. Place desired amount of eggs on top of cheese. Add bacon and then the avocado slices. Add salt and pepper to taste.

Finally, spoon some chutney on top, and then close the panini.

Cook the panini on a panini grill for about four minutes. If you don't have a panini grill, use a heavy frying pan or griddle with an equally heavy pan on top to flatten the panini. Just remember to flip the panini to brown the other side after about two minutes. (Don't forget your oven mitts!)

Remove and serve with some kettle chips and additional slices of avocado.

Sausage, Egg, and Swiss Cheese on a Toasted Croissant

You can make this sandwich ahead and pack it for a trip to the beach, game, or any event you have to travel to. It is perfect for that stay-at-home breakfast too. It is easy to make and tastes amazing.

Ingredients

4 breakfast sausage patties

4 croissant rolls

4 eggs

4 slices Swiss cheese

3 tbsp. butter, plus 2 more tbsp. to butter
    the croissants

Kosher salt and pepper

4 tbsp. mayonnaise

1 tsp. hot sauce or ketchup

½ tsp. lemon juice

Preheat oven to 375 degrees.

Fry or bake the sausage until browned, remove, and set aside. Fry the eggs in the butter as you would normally do.

Mix together the mayo, hot sauce (or ketchup), and lemon juice.

Slice and butter the croissants.

Heat a frying pan over high heat. Place each croissant buttered side down in the frying pan for only thirty seconds, and then remove from heat. Place the toasted croissants on a parchment-lined cookie sheet.

First place a sausage patty on each croissant, then a fried egg, and finally a slice of cheese. Spoon 1 tbsp. of the mayo mix on top of cheese, and fold close the croissant.

Now place each sandwich in a heated oven until the cheese begins to melt.

Remove and serve.

If it is easier, you may place the assembled croissant sandwiches in a microwave for about thirty seconds instead of the oven.

Everyone loves sliders, especially for breakfast and especially when they are egg sliders.

Ingredients

6 eggs

3 tbsp. milk, or if you prefer, half and half, crème, or water

Parker House–style rolls (or any soft dinner roll)

Salt and pepper

2 tbsp. butter, melted

Bacon bits or cooked breakfast sausage, crumbled (optional)

Crack eggs into a bowl and add milk (or liquid of your choice), salt, and pepper. If you have a small, personal-size immersion blender, use it to mix and aerate the egg mixture. If not, use a wire whisk to vigorously mix the eggs. Aerating or mixing vigorously will help to create light and fluffy sliders.

If you have a pre-molded slider pan for hamburgers, use it, or you can use standard egg molds. Place the slider pan over low-medium heat, or place the egg molds in a frying pan over the same heat.

Liberally brush molds with melted butter, especially on sides. Gently pour egg mixture into each mold, filling each mold only halfway. As eggs start to set, use a butter knife (or a very thin spatula) to loosen eggs in the mold (do this by making a circular motion around the inside of the mold and outside of the egg). Add bacon or sausage if desired (or place on top of finished slider).

Once eggs are set (about two minutes), use a fork to lift the set eggs and turn over to cook other side (about one minute more). Be careful not to brown the eggs. Be patient; you will get it.

Place your open rolls, heated or not, on a serving plate. Lift your eggs out, one at a time, and place on a roll. If you wish, you may place a slice of cheese on top.

It is really easy. Just be patient. Everyone will love your *breakfast sliders.*

The **"Don", —I mean Dad,** is <u>gonna</u> make you a breakfast sandwich "that you can't refuse". It has many great ingredients that work so well together. As in many of my recipes, you may substitute or add ingredients. This breakfast sandwich can also be served for lunch.

Ingredients

2 fried eggs (fried in 2 tbsp. olive oil, garlic, and 1/2 tsp. oregano)

3 strips bacon

1 4- to 6-inch piece of good Italian bread cut in half horizontally (or French bread, if you must)

1 clove fresh garlic, minced

2 slices each, Swiss, provolone, and mozzarella cheeses

3 slices sopressata

3 slices Genoa salami

3 slices fresh roasted pepper (or store bought)

1 tsp. oregano

¼ cup olive oil

2 leaves of fresh basil, shredded

Fry bacon until fairly crisp, set aside.

Preheat oven to 375 degrees.

Heat the quarter cup of olive oil in a small saucepan, and then add the garlic and oregano. Cook the garlic in the oil, over low heat, for about two minutes, don't let it burn. Remove from heat immediately.

Slice the bread horizontally, and spread it open. Using a basting brush or spoon, baste the bread with the garlic oil (save any extra oil). Do not saturate the bread.

Place the bread on a parchment-lined cookie sheet and put in the oven for about one minute (do not burn bread). Remove bread from oven.

Assemble *"THE DON"*, by placing the Swiss cheese first on top of the bread, then add the sopressata and salami, and then add the remaining cheeses. Top with the roasted pepper and finally the bacon.

Next place the eggs and basil on top, and drizzle with some of the reserved oil. Sprinkle with salt and pepper. Place "The Don" back in oven for less than a minute just to melt the cheese.

Texas Tacos with Longhorn Potatoes, Bacon, Cheddar Cheese, and Salsa

Tacos are a favorite every day, but they are a special favorite on game day. This taco dish is filling and delicious and will help you get through a long day at the game or just playing with the kids.

Ingredients

6 Idaho potatoes, baked

1 tsp. cayenne pepper or paprika

10 slices bacon, cooked crisp (or sausage)

8 eggs

2 cups white cheddar cheese

2 cups Monterey Jack cheese

1 jar store-bought salsa

Salt and pepper

6 store-bought soft tacos, medium size.

To prep this dish, which will also make it easier to assemble, first reheat the potatoes if made earlier. Then break up the potatoes with a fork and add the cayenne (if using; if not, use one tsp. of paprika).

Crumble the bacon.

Scramble the eggs, and keep them warm and moist.

Warm the tacos in a microwave oven.

Get your dishes ready, and place one warm taco on each dish.

Place one scoop of the potato on each taco, then a scoop of scrambled egg, some crumbled bacon, and both cheeses.

Place in a 375 degree preheated oven until the cheese begins to melt, then remove and season with salt and pepper.

Finish with a generous scoop of salsa, and serve

A favorite stop for skiers before a long day on the slopes was a quaint Vermont breakfast café very near the mountain. Among their many morning delights was a great breakfast sandwich wrapped in a taco. It was so filling and delicious and carried you all the way through the day to Happy Hour….. Oops, I mean Après' Ski time.

Ingredients

8 to 10 eggs

2 tbsp. butter

1 cup cheddar cheese, shredded

2 jalapeño peppers, finely diced (you may use a bell pepper if you prefer)

6 to 8 potatoes of your choice, boiled and diced

8 slices bacon, cooked fairly crisp

Juice from one lime

½ tsp garlic powder (or 1 garlic clove, grated)

Salt and pepper

6 soft, store bought tortillas

2 tbsp. olive or vegetable oil

Scramble the eggs in two tbsp. of butter until they are slightly firm.

In a bowl mix the diced jalapeno, lime juice, salt, pepper, garlic powder, and olive oil. Lay your tortillas out, and then scoop a generous amount of eggs in the center of each.

Next place a scoop of the diced potatoes on top.

Spoon some of the jalapeño mix on top of the potatoes, and sprinkle with a generous amount of the crumbled bacon and cheese.

By folding the sides of the tortilla in on top of each other you will create a nice, tight burrito-type sandwich.

Very lightly brush the taco with some oil. Place in a heated frying pan and cook for four to five minutes, turning over halfway through.

Serves six hungry skiers.

Frittatas

Frittatas are a great and easy breakfast favorite. They are also perfect for a delicious dinner or brunch. You can easily satisfy your family's tastes because frittatas are so versatile. You can use the Omelet Bar suggestions on page 30 for ideas on fillings or just use your imagination. Let's go step by step. You may substitute your own ingredients for ours at any time.

Ingredients

8 to 10 eggs
1/4 cup heavy cream, half and half, or milk
Kosher salt and black pepper, to taste
Choose a meat (i.e., bacon, ham,
    prosciutto, etc.)

Choose one or two veggies (i.e., onion,
    peppers, etc.)
Choose one cheese, such as Swiss,
    shredded
Add one herb, such as basil or thyme
2 tbsp. olive oil

1/4 Preheat oven to 375 degrees. In a large bowl, whisk the eggs, cream (or liquid of your choice), salt, and pepper.

Fry the bacon, and then drain on paper towels.

Lightly sauté the veggies. Once slightly cooled, add them, the bacon, and the cheese to the egg mixture and mix thoroughly.

Using a large cast iron skillet or oven-proof frying pan, heat the oil over moderate heat. Add the egg mixture to the hot oil. Pour slowly for safety. Lower the heat and cook for about ten minutes. You don't have to stir.

Use oven mitts to transfer the hot skillet to the already-heated oven, and cook until set and slightly browned (about five to eight minutes).

Again using your oven mitts, with two hands remove the skillet from the oven. Use a rounded butter knife or firm spatula to loosen the sides of the frittata from the skillet.

Gently slide the frittata from the skillet onto a cutting board.

Slice into desired pieces and serve. Hot sauce works well for those who like it. You may also want to sprinkle some grated parmesan cheese on top and serve.

Piccolino **means small or little** in Italian. These little frittatas are perfect for the kids or to serve at Brunch.

Ingredients

8 eggs

3 to 4 tbsp. half and half or milk

½ tsp. kosher salt

Butter or spray for muffin tin

½ tsp. pepper

½ cup finely diced Genoa salami

½ cup grated Parmigiano Reggiano cheese

2 tbsp. fresh basil, finely chopped

1 tbsp Italian parsley, finely chopped

Whisk together eggs, half and half, salt, pepper, salami, cheese, and herbs. Mix well.

Butter or spray the wells of a muffin tin. Pour egg mixture into cups, filling about three-quarters full.

Bake in the oven for about 8 minutes.

Slide a butter knife around the sides of the frittatas, and remove from the tin to a plate.

Garnish with parsley and serve.

Ahh! **Potatoes and eggs are** amazing. The taste of crispy potatoes, fried onions, parmesan cheese, and eggs is incredible. This dish is perfect for breakfast, lunch, or dinner, dipped in ketchup or hot sauce, or served on fresh bread or a baguette. Everyone loves potatoes and eggs.

Ingredients

4 large russet potatoes, thinly sliced, preferably on a mandolin

8 large eggs, slightly beaten

1 large yellow onion, thinly sliced

½ cup grated parmesan cheese

Salt and pepper

Vegetable oil for frying

In a large skillet, add vegetable oil (about half an inch deep). When heated, add potatoes (do in two batches if needed). Cook till golden brown on edges. Place on a cookie sheet lined with paper towels to drain. Sprinkle lightly with salt.

Next, drain most of the oil from the skillet, leaving a light coating. Add the sliced onions and cook till lightly browned. Add potatoes back into the skillet with the onions. Mix parmesan cheese to beaten eggs, and add a little black pepper. Pour over potatoes. Cook over medium heat until starting to set. You can lift edges of mixture to allow the eggs to flow into the bottom of the skillet. When almost set, flip the eggs over to brown the top. Place on platter, cut into wedges, and serve.

Ham and Swiss Frittata with Red Pepper and Olives

Ham and Swiss cheese omelets are among the favorite of egg dishes. You can add new flavor and an added dimension by adding peppers (hot if you prefer) and olives, turning the whole dish into a frittata.

Ingredients

2 tbsp. olive oil

2 tbsp. butter

1 large roasted red pepper

¼ cup each kalamata, Spanish pimiento, and black olives, chopped

6 eggs

3 tbsp. milk or half and half

1 large onion, diced

1 cup ham, diced

1 cup Swiss cheese, shredded

Black pepper

Heat the oil and butter in a large cast iron skillet or oven-proof pan. Add onion to pan and cook for about four minutes or until translucent. Add ham and olives to pan and continue to cook for one minute more, and then add roasted peppers. Mix together and continue to cook for another two minutes.

In a bowl, whisk the eggs and milk together. Add pepper to taste.

Pour eggs into the pan and stir well. Let the eggs set for about one and a half minutes. Lift and fold the eggs with a heat-proof spatula. This will allow the uncooked liquid to flow to the bottom of the pan. Continue to cook the mixture for another three minutes.

Sprinkle the cheese on top of the eggs. Transfer skillet to the oven for five to six minutes or until the cheese melts. Be careful not to burn the cheese (it should brown just a touch).

Remove from oven. With a spatula, remove the frittata to a plate, divide, and serve.

The wonderful tastes of Mediterranean cuisine are very noticeable in this frittata. To spice the frittata up a bit, you may add a quarter cup of chopped Genoa salami or Soppressata and a touch of crushed red pepper when you add the peppers and olives.

Ingredients

4 tbsp. olive oil

1 onion, diced

¼ cup each Spanish, kalamata, and black oil cured olives, chopped

1 large roasted red or pimento pepper, thinly sliced or chopped

6 eggs

3 to 4 tbsp. half and half or milk

Black pepper

Preheat oven to 375 degrees.

Heat oil in an oven-proof or cast iron skillet, add onion, and cook for about four minutes or until translucent.

Add peppers and olives to the onions, and cook for another two to three minutes.

Whisk eggs briskly with milk, and then add the pepper to taste.

Pour eggs into skillet, mixing well with onion, pepper, and olive mix.

Cook until eggs are almost set, about five minutes, and then carefully place the skillet in a heated oven for about five to six minutes.

Remove from oven and slide frittata onto a cutting board. Divide the frittata into slices and serve.

Other Breakfast Specials

Making a quiche for breakfast or brunch is as impressive as it is delicious. You can make the quiche the day before and just reheat it in the morning. You can also use store-bought crust to make this dish even easier. There are so many variations of quiches, and you can use your imagination to make quiches to suit your taste.

Ingredients

1 nine-inch, unbaked pie shell

1 egg white, lightly beaten

6 bacon slices

2 cups Swiss cheese, shredded

4 eggs

1 ½ cups half and half

½ tsp. kosher salt

Dash fresh nutmeg

¼ tsp. black pepper

Start by preheating your oven to 375 degrees.

Brush the inside of the pie shell with the egg white. This should seal any cracks that may develop in the pie crust while baking.

Fry the bacon until crispy, remove from pan, and drain on paper towels. Crumble the bacon into small pieces.

Next, whisk the eggs in a bowl, add the half and half, salt, pepper, and nutmeg, and continue to whisk until well mixed. Add the bacon to the pie shell, and then add the shredded Swiss cheese. Now pour the egg mixture over the bacon and cheese.

Place the quiche in the oven on a baking sheet on the bottom rack. Bake the quiche for thirty-five to forty minutes or until set. The top of the quiche should be golden brown. You can insert a wooden skewer into the center. It should come out clean.

Remove from the oven and let cool on a wire rack for ten minutes.

Slice and serve!

Matzo Brei is a traditional Jewish dish usually served at Passover, but it is so tasty that it may be served year round. At the end of the recipe below, I added maple syrup to bring an interesting and delicious taste to this version of Matzo Brei.

Ingredients

4 large pieces matzo (usually six-by-six inches each)

4 eggs

½ cup milk

4 tbsp. butter

Kosher salt and white pepper to taste

Maple syrup or honey

Break the matzo into small pieces, and place them in a large bowl of water for about fifteen seconds. Drain the matzo quickly. You don't want them to be soggy. Whisk the eggs, milk, salt, and pepper in a large bowl, and then add the well-drained matzo and mix well.

Melt the butter in a large skillet or frying pan over moderate heat. Add the matzo-egg mixture to the pan. Let the eggs set for one and a half to two minutes. With a heat-proof spatula, turn and fold the eggs from the bottom and sides.

Matzo Brei can be a little firmer and a little more well done than your regular scrambled eggs, but once again, cook to your personal liking. Remove from the pan and serve immediately.

To add some extra flavor, let your family or guests drizzle some maple syrup or honey over their portion of Matzo Brei. It's absolutely delicious!

You may want to add some finely chopped chives over the finished dish, or just serve as is and enjoy.

Potato pancakes add so much to any breakfast dish. They are an absolute favorite with everyone, and they are so delicious. Potato pancakes are so good that you can serve them separate, as is or as an accompaniment to eggs, pancakes, or any other breakfast dish. Add the potato pancakes to bread, bacon, and eggs and make an awesome breakfast sandwich (or Panini). Of course, don't forget them for an addition to lunch or dinner.

To spice up the potato pancakes for the adults, just sprinkle a little cayenne pepper while mixing all the ingredients together.

Ingredients

3 Yukon Gold potatoes

1 extra-large or jumbo egg, beaten

2 to 3 tbsp. all-purpose flour

3 tbsp. fresh chives, minced

1 medium onion, minced

Kosher salt and pepper to taste

2 tbsp. vegetable oil (more if needed)

Grate the potatoes coarsely and then place in a large bowl of salted water for ten to twenty minutes. Drain the potatoes in a colander and then squeeze the excess water from the potatoes with your hands, and place in a separate bowl or large dish. This will release the starchy liquid. Discard the water. Next, pat the potatoes dry with paper towels.

In a large bowl, mix the potatoes, onions, flour, chives, salt, and pepper. Make a small ball with the mixture, and then gently flatten it with your hand or spatula (about one inch thick). Repeat with the rest of the mixture.

Heat the oil in a large skillet over medium-high heat for about one and a half minutes. Place the potato pancakes, one by one, into the skillet. Use a spatula, and be careful. Let pancakes cook for about four minutes or until crispy and golden brown. Do not disturb the pancakes until you are ready to turn them over.

When one side is browned, turn the pancakes over and cook for an additional three minutes. Watch them carefully. You want the pancakes to be nice and crispy but not burned.

Remove the finished potato pancakes with a spatula and place on a paper towel to drain the oil.

Keep warm in a 200- to 225-degree oven until ready to serve. Try serving with apple sauce.

Be very careful with the hot oil. Keep the kids away from the hot pan, and turn the handle of the pan facing in.

Home Fries with Onion and Crispy Bacon

Home fries are a great match with any meal. For breakfast you can serve them as a "side". You can also serve the home fries with a fried or poached egg on top.

Home fries refrigerate well, so keep them on hand.

Ingredients

4 Idaho potatoes, unpeeled

3 tbsp. olive oil

4 strips smoked bacon, fried fairly crisp

2 onions, chopped

1 tsp. paprika

1 tsp. cayenne pepper (optional)

Kosher salt and pepper

Prick the potatoes with a fork several times and place on the center rack in a preheated oven (400 degrees). Bake for one hour, and then remove and let cool. Cut the unpeeled potatoes into fairly large cubes.

In a large bowl, mix the potatoes, olive oil, onions, salt, pepper, paprika, and cayenne (if using).

Heat a large cast iron skillet or frying pan over a medium-high heat. Add the potato mixture to the skillet and cook until brown and crispy. (Don't turn too often, for this will slow down the browning process.)

Crumble the crispy bacon into the pan and mix. Cook for five minutes more.

Remove from skillet and serve.

Good Old-Fashioned Biscuits and Gravy with Sausage Patties

Whenever we traveled south when the boys were younger, we always made it a point to have good old Southern-style biscuits and gravy for breakfast. Almost all of the restaurants in the South serve biscuits and gravy as a part of a good Southern breakfast. Now you can bring a part of the South into your kitchen by making your own biscuits and gravy. Once again, it is fast, easy, and delicious, *Y'All*.

Ingredients

2 tbsp. butter.
1 lb. bulk sausage
3 tbsp. all-purpose flour
2 cups whole milk

6 purchased buttermilk biscuits
6 purchased breakfast sausage patties (or more for a heartier breakfast)
1 tsp. salt (more to taste)
½ tsp. pepper

Heat a large skillet over medium heat, melt the butter, and then add the bulk sausage. As the sausage begins to brown, break it up in the skillet with a heat-proof spatula or wooden spoon. Cook the sausage for five minutes or until browned. Remove cooked sausage to a dish, leaving all of the drippings in the skillet

Place the sausage patties in the same pan and cook on both sides until brown (about ten minutes). Remove patties from the skillet, and keep warm in a separate dish.

Next add the flour to the skillet, stirring for about one minute. Add the milk, salt, and pepper and stir or whisk for another two and a half minutes.

The gravy should begin to thicken. Add the cooked bulk sausage and juice from the dish back to the skillet. Stir for another one and a half minutes.

Heat the biscuits in the oven or microwave and then slice in half. Place the open biscuit on a plate. Place a sausage patty on top of the heated biscuit, and pour some of that beautiful gravy on top. You may want to sprinkle with a little more pepper.

Ingredients

4 russet potatoes
1/2 cup onions, chopped
½ tsp. salt

¼ tsp. pepper
4 tbsp. butter or corn oil

Start by cutting the potatoes into quarters. Now chop the quarters into cubes. Place the potatoes into a saucepan with boiling water (enough to cover potatoes) and boil for about five to seven minutes. When finished, remove potatoes and drain.

In a large bowl, combine potatoes, onion, ½ tsp. salt, and pepper, and mix.

Melt the butter in a cast iron skillet or large frying pan over medium heat. Add the potatoes and onions, and raise the heat to medium-high and cook for twenty to twenty-five minutes. Don't disturb too often, turning only occasionally. You want a brown crust.

Place in serving bowl.

Note: To spice it up a bit, you may add some diced peppers of your choice or a dash of cayenne pepper when you add the onions.

Pizza Fritta is also known as fried dough. At just about any amusement park or county fair you will find pizza fritta. Most people love it with sugar while others prefer it with tomato sauce. Then there are those who love their pizza fritta just plain! Now you can enjoy it at home. All you need is a fairly deep frying pan or an electric skillet, some vegetable oil, some dough, and you're good to go.

Ingredients

1 to 2 lbs. store-bought pizza dough (preferably from a pizza shop)

1 quart corn oil (more if needed; you want the dough to float in the oil)

½ cup all-purpose flour

Remove the dough from the refrigerator and let rest for a least one hour (if frozen, let it rest overnight).

Lightly flour the dough and your work surface.

Cut dough into approximately three-inch by three-inch pieces. Then gently stretch each piece (try not make holes in the dough).

Pour oil into a large skillet over high heat. When oil is *hot* and area is secured for safety, place as many pieces of the dough into the oil as you can fit without overcrowding (use tongs). Fry the dough until golden, and then gently turn over to fry the other side for another two to three minutes. Repeat process with remaining dough, placing finished pieces on paper towels to drain any excess oil.

To serve, place a piece of the *pizza fritta* on a plate. You may choose any or all of the following items to flavor the *pizza fritta*.

- Sugar
- Butter
- Maple syrup
- Jelly
- Tomato sauce
- Or any of your favorite toppings, or just eat it plain.

Remember to make plenty; they are great as leftovers to pick on later.

Everyone will love your Pizza Fritta Lunga, so make plenty.

Ingredients

1 to 2 lbs. store-bought pizza dough
  (preferably from a pizza shop)
1 quart corn oil (more if needed; you want
  the dough to float in the oil)
1/2 cup all-purpose flour

1 cup granulated sugar
2 tbsp. cinnamon (more or less, to your
  taste; you do not want the cinnamon to
  overpower the sugar)

Remove dough from refrigerator and let rest for at least one hour (if frozen, let rest overnight). Lightly flour the dough. Slice dough into approximately one-inch by four-inch-long pieces.

When using hot oil, first secure area for safety. Then, place several pieces of the lunga dough into the hot oil using a pair of tongs. You want the finished pieces to be light and fluffy, so keep rolling the frying dough with your tongs. This will prevent any one side from over cooking.

Keep in hot oil for about three minutes or until golden in color. Do not overcook.

Place a paper towel on a dish. As each piece of dough is finished, remove and place on the dish to remove any excess oil.

In a large glass dish or aluminum pan, mix the sugar and cinnamon.

Place about four pieces of the finished, hot *fritta lunga* at a time into the sugar mixture and coat heavily. Remove excess sugar. Place on a dish and serve.

You're in for a real treat!

Tops in Toppings

Special toppings for your eggs, pancakes, waffles, or any other of your special dishes will add so much flavor, fun, and excitement to your breakfast or brunch. In many cases, these toppings or spreads can be used separately for toast, bagels, or crackers. The next few pages contain several recipes for spreads, sugars, butters, syrups, sauces, compotes, and glazes.

Raisin Rum Cream Cheese Spread

Ingredients

8 oz. cream cheese, softened
½ cup raisins (golden raisins preferred)
1 tbsp. granulated sugar
½ cup light brown sugar

Pinch of grated nutmeg.
1 tsp. cinnamon
½ cup rum

Place the raisins, rum and granulated sugar in a small saucepan over low heat for ten minutes.

Remove from heat, let cool for ten minutes, and then drain well.

Mix the cream cheese with a heavy spoon, spatula, or hand mixer until smooth. Then add the brown sugar, nutmeg, and cinnamon. Mix well.

Add the cooled raisins, and continue to mix until completely blended.

Refrigerate for up to one week.

The Rum Raisin spread is amazing on pancakes, waffles, bagels or toast.

Blueberry Cream Cheese Spread

Ingredients

8 oz. cream cheese, softened
¼ tsp. salt

¼ cup blueberry jam, jelly, or preserves

Place softened cream cheese in a medium-size bowl. Gently fold in salt and jam (jelly or preserves) with a spatula or wooden spoon until completely blended. Add a small dollop of the jam on top of the spread. Refrigerate until ready to use.

You can substitute the blueberry jam with strawberry jam, lemon curd, orange marmalade, or any other jam of your choice.

Maple Syrup Cream Cheese Spread

Using the above recipe, substitute quarter cup of maple syrup instead of the jam and mix well. You can add as much syrup to your particular taste.

Go slowly as you add the syrup, and taste often.

Vanilla Maple Sugar Syrup

Ingredients

1 cup maple syrup
4 tbsp. unsalted butter

1 tbsp. vanilla extract (or use 2 vanilla beans, scrape out seeds, discard shell)

In a small saucepan, add syrup, butter, and vanilla extract (or vanilla beans). Stir slowly until well blended. Simmer over medium heat for five minutes. Serve over pancakes, waffles, pizza fritta, or ice cream.

This syrup is a bit unusual but very tasty. You can add a tropical flair to your breakfast or brunch by adding this syrup. You may also substitute guava or strawberries as your fruit.

Ingredients

2 mangoes, peeled and chopped

2 papayas, peeled and chopped

1 tsp. fresh lime juice

1 cup simple syrup (½ cup water, ½ cup granulated sugar)

After you peel and chop the fruit, place in a blender, and blend until smooth. Remove the fruit from the blender and place in a strainer. Place strained fruit into a large bowl.

Meanwhile, make the simple syrup by adding equal parts of sugar and water to a saucepan. Bring to a boil over high heat until the sugar is completely dissolved, stirring as you go. Cool slightly, add the fruit and lime juice, and then stir together.

Use immediately or refrigerate up to 3 days.

You can be very creative with these syrups by substituting or adding your favorite ingredients.

Once again, go slowly and taste often.

Sugars

These sugar mixtures are so versatile. They can be used on cereals, granola, pancakes, waffles, and of course, on pizza fritta (fried dough).

Brown Sugar "Sugar"

Ingredients

2 cups brown sugar
1 ½ cups granulated sugar

2 tbsp. cinnamon

Mix all ingredients well and serve.

Cinnamon Sugar

Ingredients

2 cups fine granulated sugar (regular granulated sugar is okay too)

4 tbsp. cinnamon

Mix together. The color of this sugar after mixing thoroughly should be very light beige. If you like the taste of more cinnamon, you can certainly add more; just do it gradually. This sugar works particularly well on pizza fritta.

White Sugar Glaze

This glaze is the perfect topping for muffins, cookies, pancakes, waffles, and cakes. It is very easy to make. The consistency should not be too thick because it hardens quickly. You can adjust the consistency by the amount of milk you use. You may also use water instead of milk.

Ingredients

1/3 cup milk (you can gradually add a little more if a thinner consistency is desired)

1 cup confectioners' sugar

Whisk together until smooth, and use immediately.

Strawberry banana compote can be used as a side with everything you make for breakfast. It is great on top of toast, bagels, waffles, and pound cake.

Ingredients

2 cups fresh or frozen strawberries, sliced   ½ cup soft brown sugar

1 cup sliced bananas   Juice of 2 oranges

Zest of 1 lime and 1 orange   ½ tsp. cinnamon

Place the brown sugar, orange juice, lime and orange zest, and cinnamon in a saucepan. Heat over medium heat until the sugar is dissolved. Add the strawberries, and bring to a boil. Gently stir in the bananas.

Remove the pan from the heat immediately, and pour compote into heat-proof bowl to cool slightly.

Serve warm or at room temperature.

Ingredients

2 cups fresh or frozen strawberries
(thawed)

2 cups fresh or frozen mixed berries
(thawed)

2 tbsp. maple syrup

1/3 cup finely granulated sugar

½ cup orange juice

2 tbsp. lemon juice

Combine berries, sugar, orange, and lemon juices in a nonreactive saucepan over medium heat. Simmer for five minutes, stirring very gently (taste to see if you need to add more maple syrup).

Remove from heat, let cool slightly, and then serve over crepes, pancakes, or waffles.

Fantastic, Creamy Flavored Butters

Maple Syrup Butter

Ingredients

½ cup unsalted butter, softened

4 tbsp. maple syrup

Mix together until completely blended. Serve immediately, or refrigerate up to five days.

Very Berry Butter

Ingredients

½ cup unsalted butter, softened
¼ cup confectioners' sugar or
    granulated sugar

1/2 cup finely diced fresh strawberries or
    1/4 cup strawberry preserves

Combine all ingredients and blend well. Serve immediately or refrigerate up to three days. You can substitute or combine any berries to your liking. You can also adjust the amount of sugar to your particular taste. Combine slowly and taste often.

Orange Zest Butter

Ingredients

½ cup unsalted butter, softened
3 tbsp. confectioners' or granulated sugar

1 tbsp. grated orange zest
½ tsp. cinnamon

Combine all ingredients until well blended. Once again, you can add more sugar or zest to your taste.

Hollandaise sauce is perfect over Eggs Benedict. It is a luxuriously delicious sauce that your family or guests will love. You may want to use it on other egg dishes as well.

Ingredients

4 egg yolks
3 tbsp. freshly squeezed lemon juice
2 sticks unsalted butter, melted

Pinch of salt and black pepper
½ tsp. cayenne pepper
1 tsp. chopped tarragon

Place the egg yolks, lemon juice, cayenne, salt and pepper into a blender at low speed. Slowly drizzle the melted butter into the still-running blender. If the sauce thickens too much, slowly, add a little water (about 1 tbsp. until desired texture is achieved).

Don't be impatient; just go slowly and taste as you go for seasoning.

When the sauce is completed, pour into a small serving bowl, add tarragon, and serve immediately.

Beverages

Just a Few Morning Beverages

It really isn't necessary to serve elaborate drinks to your family or friends for breakfast, but it can be lots of fun. Orange juice or cranberry juice usually works just fine, especially for quick breakfasts. Dad has chosen a few drinks to serve that are very easy to prepare. Some have alcohol for your adult guests and some, of course, do not. We used to serve a drink that we called "Magnolia Sunrise", which we adapted for our family (no alcohol for the kids) that was named for the street we lived on at the time.

You can do the same thing and let the kids name it. The name and the drink will last forever, being passed down for years. If you are serving brunch, it is nice to have something special to drink, so here are a few ideas.

Magnolia Sunrise

(Rename it for your family if you choose.)

Ingredients

4 oz. fresh orange juice

1 oz. Amaretto

½ oz. grenadine

Orange slice for garnish

Pour the orange juice into a nice juice or champagne glass. Add the Amaretto, the grenadine, and then the orange garnish. Omit the Amaretto and add a little more grenadine for the children.

Our boys loved it and now serve Magnolia Sunrises to their families.

Ingredients

2 oz. Champagne or other sparkling wine   Orange slices for garnish
2 oz. fresh orange juice

Pour champagne or wine into champagne or long, thin glasses. Add the orange juice and orange slice to garnish. You can use any clear soda or tonic instead of Champagne for the kids.

You can also add half an ounce of Triple Sec to the drink for the adults.

Ingredients

1 oz. vodka

6 to 8 oz. of tomato or V-8 juice

1 tsp. fresh lemon juice

1 tsp. fresh lime juice

½ tsp. salt (more or less to taste)

½ tsp. pepper

1 to 2 tsp. Worcestershire sauce

A few dashes of Tabasco sauce (optional)

Ice

Add all ingredients to a cocktail shaker and mix well. Taste then add more salt and pepper, to taste.

The new trend is to add one tsp. of horseradish to the drink.

Pour into a tall glass; use a slice of lemon or lime for garnish. To be real fancy, add a celery stalk.

For the kids, leave out the vodka and hot sauce.

Ingredients

3 oz. Champagne or sparkling wine   1 strawberry for garnish
1 small sugar cube

Pour champagne into a tall, fluted champagne glass

Drop the sugar cube into the glass, and garnish with a strawberry.

Ingredients

2 tbsp. Nutella (chocolate hazelnut spread, available in supermarkets)

1 cup hot chocolate

Whipped cream or Cool Whip

1 tsp. cocoa powder

Pour hot chocolate into a large cup. Add Nutella, and stir well.

Top with whipped cream or Cool Whip. Sprinkle chocolate powder on top to finish.

Adults may substitute coffee for hot chocolate and add a splash of vanilla vodka or Kahlua.

Dads Do Breakfast **took three** years to write, but it took a lifetime of experiences to fill the pages. *Dads Do Breakfast* is filled with incredible memories of the days when Renee and I raised our three sons. In actuality I think they raised me as much as I raised them. They were great years filled with fun and so much love that it is hard to express.

My special thanks go to my three sons, Tony, Brandon, and Daryl, for being the most incredible sons a dad could hope for. I thank them for their help in editing this book, for their sound advice and enthusiasm, and also for creating the great memories as they grew up and the laughter and fun they provided at our breakfast table. Incidentally, they are great dads to their children and amazing cooks in their own right.

Thanks to my daughters-in-law, Rouxle, Michele, and Chelsea. Aside from being more like daughters to me, they provided great and constant encouragement for this book.

To my son Daryl and his wife, Chelsea, you are absolutely incredible. Thank you for the countless hours you spent editing and improving the format for *Dads Do Breakfast*.

Then there are Malia, Taylor, Kaia, Arianna, Kenna, and Olivia, the greatest grandchildren on earth and my special taste testers. (Kids always tell the truth!)

And of course, special thanks and gratitude to the light of my life, my wife, Renee, for all the time and effort she spent making *Dads Do Breakfast* become a reality. Thank you for helping to "unscramble" my thoughts and keeping them in order. Renee helped to make each recipe so much better. Her insight and editing talents were priceless.

A special note of thanks to my family as a whole—thank you for the inspiration, enthusiasm, and loyalty. I love you all so much.

Finally, one last thought. Remember, we are not gourmet chefs. We are dads doing our best to make a great breakfast for our families and friends in a fun, love-filled, and happy environment. *Now that's family!*

CPSIA information can be obtained
at www.ICGtesting.com
Printed in the USA
BVXC01n2123150514
353427BV00004BA/1